Mammals which live in the wa[...] *in that some forty-five millio*[...] *which were land-based mamma*[...] *of life. Perhaps, in order to esc*[...] *their food more easily, they gradually deserted the land and took to the waters or the air. Perhaps changes in the earth's climate and in their environment made it necessary to find a new habitat and adopt a new element. This changed way of life was very gradual and took millions of years to accomplish.*

Whales and, to a lesser degree, seals gradually altered their whole physical make-up. Limbs, breathing systems, blood supply, body chemistry, eyes, ears, bone structure all altered.

Bats evolved new shapes and found new ways of finding their way about and detecting their prey.

But all these transformed animals retain to this day the essential characteristics of mammals. Most of them still retain at least some vestiges of hair; all of them produce young in a true mammalian fashion and feed them on milk from the mammary glands from which mammals get their name. They have back-bones and are warm-blooded and most of them are intelligent.

There are millions of seals and bats in the world and the oceans contain vast numbers of whales and dolphins. And yet, because they may be nocturnal, or because their habitat is normally so remote from our own, we know relatively little about them.

Whales and seals have suffered terribly from man's greed and have been over-hunted to the point where some species are dangerously reduced. We must do all that we can to ensure their survival.

A Ladybird Book
Series 691

'Sea and Air Mammals' is the seventh
of a Ladybird series of books about animals
of the world. The superb full-colour
illustrations by John Leigh-Pemberton,
the well known bird and animal painter, are
supported by an informative text and a
colourful end paper showing the distribution
of these mammals. An index is given and
also, at the back, a chart showing the
various Orders and Families to which the
animals belong.

SEA and AIR MAMMALS

written and illustrated by
JOHN LEIGH-PEMBERTON

Ladybird Books Ltd Loughborough

Northern Fur Seal
(*Bull above, cow and pup below*)

Length, head and body:
Bull 200 cm.   Cow 150 cm.

Weight: Bull up to 300 Kg.
                      Cow up to 68 Kg.

All seals (order *Pinnipedia*) are descended from an original carnivore stock and are divided into three families. *Otariidae*, the 'Eared' seals, have small external ears and hind flippers which can be directed forwards, thus enabling the animal to be moderately agile on land. The *Phocidae*, or True Seals, have no external ears and their hind flippers, which are nothing more than specially adapted hind legs, cannot be directed forwards. They are thus somewhat clumsy on shore. The third family contains but one species, the Walrus (*Odobenidae*) whose hind flippers can be directed forwards.

Altogether there are thirty-one species, some of which are becoming extremely rare. It is thought that *Otariidae* may be descended from a stock similar to the Bears and that *Phocidae* come from the same source as Otters. But in spite of their differing origins all seals look very much alike, a fact deriving from the similarity of their way of life.

Typical of the *Otariidae* is the Northern Fur Seal which breeds in the Pribilof Islands in the Bering Sea and is found throughout the North Pacific Ocean during winter. They spend most of their lives in the water, but come ashore in large colonies to breed in June and July.

Like the other Fur Seals of the world, such as the Australian and South American species, they have been greatly over-hunted for their fur and were once in grave danger of extinction. Now, thanks to protection, their numbers have increased to nearly two million animals. The total world population of Fur Seals is probably in the region of four million.

0 7214 0319 0

Patagonian Sea Lion
(*top*)

Length, head and body:
Bull 235 cm.   Cow 180 cm.

Steller's Sea Lion
(*centre*)

Length, head and body:
Bull 350 cm.   Cow 270 cm.

California Sea Lion
(*bottom*)

Length, head and body:
Bull 245 cm.   Cow 190 cm.

Because they are animals which live almost entirely in the water Seals have evolved so that they are fully adapted to their way of life. Their shape is streamlined, their limbs specially modified for swimming and their internal organs adapted to such activities as deep, prolonged dives or drinking only sea water. Their eyes are highly efficient under water and in very poor light; and their skin and thick layer of blubber protect them from the intense cold in which most of them live.

Sea Lions (family *Otariidae*) are really Fur Seals which have only one layer of fur, while Fur Seals have an under coat as well as the coarse outer hairs. Sea Lions are found in sub-tropical waters as well as in the colder areas near the polar regions.

Patagonian Sea Lions occur from Brazil to the Strait of Magellan and in the Pacific up to Peru. Steller's Sea Lion is found in the North Pacific from Japan and California as far north as the Bering Sea. The bulls of both these species are massive, heavily maned animals, the cows being very much smaller. Bulls grunt and roar and in the breeding season gather 'harems' of cows, showing great aggression.

California Sea Lions are those in circuses and zoos. They occur in sub-tropical waters of the Pacific along the western coast of North America, in Japan and in the Galapagos Islands. They move quite well on land and their bark or 'hoot' is a familiar sound in zoos. Other species of Sea Lion occur in Australia and New Zealand. The total world population is about one million.

Common or Harbour Seal
Bull (*top*), Cow (*centre*),
Pup (*bottom*)

Length, head and body:
up to 195 cm.
Length, head and body:
up to 165 cm.
Length at birth   up to 90 cm.

The word '*Pinnipedia*' means literally 'Feather-footed', referring to the fore-limbs or flippers. It is these that the *Otariidae* use chiefly for swimming, while the *Phocidae* tend to use their hind limbs. But all seals also use the whole body in swimming and in their extremely acrobatic manoeuvres under water. On land the *Otariidae* can use their hind legs but other seals have to hump themselves along somewhat awkwardly. Most seals when swimming can jump clear of the water and some species can attain speeds of about 15 knots.

All seals are carnivores, living on fish, shell-fish, squid and minute marine shrimps. Some seals eat sea birds and small whales and others are partly cannibals.

Of all the True Seals (family *Phocidae*) the Common or Harbour Seals are typical. They are found in the northern hemisphere, usually in salt water but sometimes in rivers and even in a few freshwater lakes. In Europe they occur chiefly on the Scandinavian coasts and on the eastern coast of Scotland. They prefer sandbanks and shallow estuaries and live in small groups which break up in summer and reform after the mating season in September.

One or two pups are born after a gestation period of 280 days. At birth they have a white, fluffy coat which they lose almost immediately (sometimes before they are born). They can swim at once, unlike members of the *Otariidae* which have not sufficient blubber to provide protection or buoyancy until they are several weeks old.

Common Seals are preyed upon by Polar Bears and by Killer Whales, but apart from this can live for nearly twenty years.

Bearded Seal (*top*)	*Length, head and body:* *Bull up to 325 cm.* *Cow up to 250 cm.*
Ringed Seal (*centre*)	*Length, head and body:* *Bull up to 160 cm. Cow similar.*
Grey Seal (*bottom*)	*Length, head and body:* *Bull up to 300 cm.* *Cow up to 225 cm.*

Many seals, living in polar regions, have to be able to exist on ice at temperatures as low as —40°C. Their own body temperature must be maintained at about 37.5°C (99.9°F) and this is partly achieved by the protective layer of blubber or oily fat beneath the skin. This accounts for as much as a quarter of their total weight.

Seals must be able to hunt for food below the ice, and accordingly they create holes in the ice through which they can dive or rise to the surface to breathe. They can stay submerged for up to twenty minutes and can dive to as much as 150 metres or more. They create holes by gnawing with their teeth and keep them open in the same way and by constant use.

Seals of the Arctic regions include the rather rare Bearded Seal which occurs from the polar ice-pack to Norway, Japan and Newfoundland. It feeds on the sea bottom, mostly on shell-fish, and is much hunted by Eskimos for its fat and leather.

Probably the commonest seal is the Ringed Seal, found all over the Arctic to the North Pole, much hunted by man, Polar Bear and Killer Whale. The world population of this species may be as high as five million.

The Grey Seal is found in more temperate waters of the North Atlantic and is commonest on rocky coasts of western Britain and in the Baltic. There is also a western population centred on the Gulf of St. Lawrence. The British group breeds in the autumn and the others in winter.

Crabeater Seal *(bottom)*	*Length, head and body:*	*260 cm.*
Weddell Seal *(top)*	*Length, head and body:*	*300 cm.*
Leopard Seal *(centre)*	*Length, head and body:*	*350 cm.*

The Antarctic and southern oceans have their own species of seals which differ in some ways from the northern seals. There are four species, in all of which the females are larger than the males. Most of them have particularly large eyes, and teeth specialised for their type of diet.

Ross Seals (not shown) are a little known species which occurs only on the pack-ice surrounding Antarctica. Until quite recently only a few had ever been seen. They are believed to be solitary animals which do not winter beneath the pack-ice and are particularly rapid swimmers.

The world population of Crabeater Seals is estimated at about five million. However, estimating seal populations is almost impossible as they live mostly in such remote, inaccessible and often unexplored places. Crabeaters have extraordinary teeth, not for eating crabs but for straining 'krill', minute shrimp-like creatures which form their principal diet. Of all seals this is the fastest mover on land.

The Weddell Seal, like the Crabeater, ranges from the Antarctic to the shores of Australia, New Zealand and southern South America. This heavy, rather tame animal is the seal most often seen in southern waters. Much of the winter is spent on ice-shelves below the ice. New-born pups are nearly half the length of their mother and weigh about 30 Kg.

The Leopard Seal is distributed around Antarctica and occurs occasionally in other southern areas. This is a savage seal with large jaws and fearsome teeth. It is the only seal which habitually preys on sea birds, penguins and other seals.

Walrus

Length, head and body:
Bull 370 cm.   Weight 1300 Kg.
Cows about ⅓ smaller.

The Walrus (family *Odobenidae*) inhabits the Arctic Ocean in areas near the limit of the polar ice, extending to Siberia, Alaska and Greenland. These animals migrate as the ice advances in winter, returning as the ice retreats in spring. In spite of their great bulk they can travel over land or across snow.

Herds of about a hundred congregate on rocky islands, lying packed together in the sun and frequently getting blistered and sunburnt. Both sexes grow long tusks which reach 100 cm. on bulls and about 60 cm. on cows. These tusks are used for various purposes such as digging on the sea bed, hauling themselves out of the water onto the ice and, occasionally, for fighting.

Food consists of shell-fish, some seaweed, small whales or seals; but in spite of its size the Walrus has a very small stomach and can eat only limited amounts at a time. To obtain shell-fish, Walruses dive to about ninety metres and their 'moustaches' consist of sensitive hairs which help them to find objects in the dark at such depths.

Hearing and sense of smell are rather poor, but Walruses have quite good eyesight and very loud voices, similar to the baying of a large dog or even the trumpeting of an elephant.

The single pup is carried on its mother's neck both on land and in water until it is able to fend for itself. This may be as much as two years, during which time the mother continues to suckle it.

Walruses have been extensively hunted for flesh, hide and ivory, and their numbers are steadily decreasing.

Northern Elephant Seal (top)

Length, head and body:
Bull 600 cm.   Cow 350 cm.

Harp Seal (centre left; male above, female and pup below)

Length, head and body: 180 cm.

Hooded Seal (bottom; cow and pup left, bull right)

Length, head and body:
Bull 350 cm.   Cow 300 cm.

There are two species of Elephant Seals (family *Phocidae*), the southern from Argentina and the southern oceans, and the northern which inhabits the coast of California, sometimes wandering as far north as British Columbia. These are the largest seals, huge animals which can dive to great depths and swim very rapidly.

During the breeding season (December to March for the northern species) enormous herds are formed on rocky shores, and during this time they do not feed. Bulls collect 'harems' of cows which produce single pups after a gestation period of 350 days. In winter the herds disperse, living entirely at sea.

Harp Seals inhabit the North Atlantic and are migratory. These and the rather similar Ribbon Seals of the North Pacific are the only seals where males and females are differently coloured. Single pups are born on the ice in March and are suckled for ten days by the mother on the exceptionally rich milk which all seals give. During this time the pup gains weight by about 2 Kg. a day and, when weaned, is left to fend for itself. For about fourteen days it does not feed and grows a new coat. It then takes to the sea, forms herds and migrates northwards.

Like the Elephant Seal, the Hooded Seal has a bladder on the nose which can be inflated when the animal is angry. Possessed by both sexes, it is largest in the male.

Hooded Seals, occurring on the ice-pack of the North Atlantic and Arctic Oceans, are migratory. Their pups are much in demand by seal hunters for their beautiful 'blue' pelt.

Baikal Seal

Length, head and body:
about 100 cm.

The Ringed Seal, one of the most numerous in the world, has several close relatives who have adapted to a life spent entirely in fresh water. Many seals will inhabit estuaries or even swim some way up rivers, but they are primarily marine (salt-water) mammals.

However, in Lake Baikal in the Soviet Union, to the north of Mongolia, is found a species which must have been isolated there many centuries ago and has adapted to a fresh water life. Lake Baikal, which is not connected in any way with the sea, freezes over in winter, and Baikal Seals are very much seals of the ice, following it northwards in summer and congregating on rocky islets in groups (or 'rookeries' as groups of seals are rather unexpectedly called).

Only the pregnant cows winter on the ice, all the others spend the whole of their time in the water where they create and maintain breathing holes. They feed entirely on small fish.

Like the Ringed Seal, the Baikal Seal is much hunted, every part of it being of use. Between five and ten thousand are killed every year out of a total population of from forty to one hundred thousand.

Other seals of the same type occur in the Caspian Sea, which is only slightly salt and freezes only in its northern half. This huge inland sea supports over a million seals. Fresh water seals also occur in smaller numbers in Lake Saimaa in Finland and in Lake Ladoga in Russia. The latter sometimes swim up the River Neva as far as Leningrad.

Mediterranean Monk Seal

Length, head and body:
about 300 cm.

One of the most curious facts about seals is the way in which they breathe. A mammal which dives for its food must have special facilities for spending long periods without breathing, which is what a seal does. When diving they take only a small amount of air into their lungs, and even on land they can go for about ten minutes without breathing. They can even sleep while submerged.

Most seals inhabit the colder waters round the poles. But some Sea Lions, Fur Seals and Elephant Seals extend to temperate regions, and there is one interesting sub-family of true seals (*Phocidae*) which is found in tropical parts of the world. These are the Monk Seals (sub-family *Monachinae**). There are three very similar species, all of them rare and very widely separated geographically.

The Hawaiian Monk Seal occurs chiefly on Laysan Island, Hawaii, with a population of about fifteen hundred animals. The Caribbean Monk Seal may already be extinct, but was once found in Jamaican waters. This was the first New World mammal to be found by Columbus' sailors, who slaughtered it for food.

Mediterranean Monk Seals are also declining in numbers and there may be fewer than five hundred left. They live in small colonies in the Black Sea, the Adriatic, along the north west coast of Africa and in the Canary Islands. They have always been persecuted by fishermen and in recent years the caves in which they breed have been discovered by skin-divers, who frighten them away. Monk Seals breed only in alternate years and produce pups which are jet black at birth.

* Note: Family names end in -I*DAE*, sub-family names in -I*NAE*.

Sea Otter

Length, head and body: 110 cm.
Length of tail: 30 cm.
Weight: up to 35 Kg.

Some mammals, although not fully adapted to an aquatic life, are partially so and are more at home in the water than on land. The Hippopotamus* and the Polar Bear** are obvious examples. Otters, too, are of course largely aquatic and the most aquatic of this family (*Mustelidae*) is the Sea Otter of the Californian and Alaskan coasts.

Sea Otters have webbed hind feet, special teeth to deal with their diet of clams, crabs and fish, and a thick under-fur to protect them from water.

But they have no special adaptations for diving to the extent that seals have, and no layer of blubber under the skin. Almost their whole lives are spent at sea, usually among seaweed beds. They mate and breed in the sea and sleep floating on their backs and anchored to a strand of seaweed.

Pups, born singly after a gestation period of up to nine months are carried on their mother's chest for a few weeks. At birth they are very developed for a carnivore although they are suckled for about a year.

When the Sea Otter feeds it dives to the sea bed, usually no more than 40 metres, collects its food and picks up a flat stone. It then rises to the surface, floats on its back and, using the stone as a sort of anvil, batters its hard-shelled food against it until the shell is broken.

Usually living in herds, Sea Otters were once almost ex-terminated on account of their fur, considered to be the most valuable in the world. Thanks to protection, they are now increasing in numbers.

* See 'African Mammals' in this series.
** See 'North American Mammals' in this series.

Common Dolphin

Length: 1·5–2·5 metres.

Whales, Dolphins and Porpoises belong to the order *Cetacea*, which contains ten families and ninety-two species. The order is divided into two sub-orders, the *Odontoceti*, or 'toothed' whales, and the *Mysticeti* or Baleen (whale-bone) whales. Dolphins are merely small whales with a 'beak' or pointed snout. Porpoises have blunt snouts. Even the smallest of them is quite a large animal.

The *Cetacea* are by far the most aquatic of all mammals and have been very markedly adapted to their way of life. Their fore-limbs have become flippers, their hind limbs have disappeared, they have a horizontal tail, no proper neck bones, no sweat glands and no hair. The whole animal is encased in a thick mass of oily blubber and the nostrils are placed in the top of the head.

One of the most familiar of all whales is the Common Dolphin, a marvellous swimmer which can leap clear of the water and travel as fast as 25 knots.

Dolphins are usually seen in groups ('schools') of anything from twenty to several hundred animals. They feed principally on fish, particularly those found near the surface. Like nearly all the toothed whales they have a great many teeth (in some species more than any other mammal). They are inquisitive, unaggressive and intelligent.

Young Dolphins are born under water after a gestation period of about nine months and are at once pushed to the surface to breathe by the mother. They are suckled, also under water, for about eighteen months.

The Common Dolphins' range is almost world-wide, including British waters, chiefly in the south and west.

Amazon Dolphin (*two forms*) (A)　　　Length: 300 cm.

Ganges Dolphin (B)　　　Length: 350 cm.

River Dolphin (D)　　　Length: 160 cm.

Bottle-nosed Dolphin (E)　　　Length: 360 cm.

Common Porpoise with calf (F)　　　Length: 150 cm.

Asiatic Finless Porpoise (C)　　　Length: 150 cm.

Some Dolphins are found only in fresh water or in the estuaries of large rivers. They are separated in a family, *Platanistidae*, and are found in India, China and South America. They are not as active as sea Dolphins of the family *Delphinidae* and feed on fish found on the muddy bottoms of rivers. In all of them the sense of sight is very poor, the Ganges Dolphin, for instance, being almost blind. They therefore use their sensitive snouts to probe for food. One species (the La Plata River Dolphin, not shown) has up to 220 teeth and the other species up to 130. These teeth, as in nearly all whales, are shaped for grasping and not for chewing or tearing; and in fact toothed whales swallow their prey whole.

The Amazon Dolphin, which occurs in two colour phases, inhabits the river system connecting the Amazon and Orinoco rivers. Like other Dolphins of this family the back (dorsal) fin is merely a ridge.

The Ganges Dolphin, from the rivers of northern India, has a slender snout and curious bony plates on each side of the skull. It lives all its life in fresh water.

The River Dolphin (family *Stenidae*) inhabits South American rivers and coasts. Unlike other freshwater Dolphins it has a distinct dorsal fin.

Bottle-nosed Dolphins (*Delphinidae*), distributed throughout the seas of the world, are those commonly seen in zoos.

The Common Porpoise ranges from the Arctic to the Antarctic and occurs in four species. Common in British waters, it is replaced in the Far East by the Finless Black Porpoise.

26

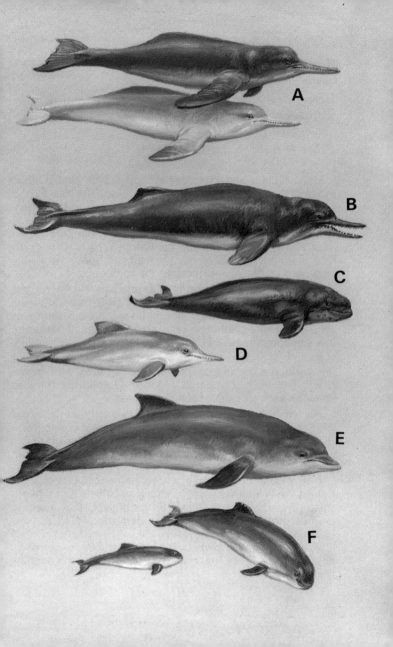

Risso's Dolphin (*top*)	*Length:*	*up to 400 cm.*
Narwhal and calf (*centre above*)	*Length:* *Tusk:*	*up to 500 cm.* *up to 250 cm.*
Beluga (White Whale) and calf (*centre below*)	*Length:*	*up to 400 cm.*
Pilot Whale (*bottom*)	*Length:*	*up to 800 cm.*

Most Whales and Dolphins are gregarious, that is, they live together in groups. All of them have to rise to the surface of the water to breathe, and when they do so they expel the used, warm air from their lungs through the 'blow-hole' in the top of the head. Toothed whales (the *Odontoceti*) have a single hole and the Baleen Whales (the *Mysticeti*) a double one. The escaping air, or 'spout', is visible because it condenses on meeting the colder air.

Large whales dive to depths of as much as 900 metres and stay submerged for over an hour. But Dolphins rise to the surface every few minutes. Before diving, a fresh supply of air is taken into the lungs, but only in very small amounts; it is sometimes expelled completely.

Risso's Dolphin (*Delphinidae*), distributed throughout the world, is a big animal often marked by long, white scars. It has few teeth, compared to other Dolphins – three to seven on each side of the lower jaw only.

Narwhals have even fewer teeth – two only, in the upper jaw; the left tooth grows through the upper lip to form the long, spiralled tusk. Narwhals (family *Monodontidae*) are confined to the Arctic Ocean. They have no dorsal fin at all.

In the same family and from the same region comes the Beluga or White Whale, the young of which looks like a small Narwhal. Very acrobatic swimmers, they make a curious bird-like sound and are often referred to as 'sea-canaries'.

Pilot Whales (*Delphinidae*) occur world-wide except in polar regions. They are extensively hunted by the whaling fleets.

Cuvier's Beaked Whale (*top*) (*two colour phases*)	Length:	up to 8·5 m.
Bottle-nosed Whale (*centre above*)	Length:	up to 9·5 m.
Killer Whale (*centre below*)	Length:	up to 8 m.
Sperm Whale (*bottom*)	Length:	up to 18 m.

Whales swim by an up and down motion of their tails or 'flukes', their front flippers being used mostly for steering. The whole body, covered with blubber which can be 30 cm. thick in some species, is adapted in a most complex way to withstand the enormous pressures experienced in a deep dive. Sometimes even the largest whales will leap clear of the water on surfacing and this is known as 'breaching'.

Whales have grown to their huge size largely because, being aquatic, they do not have to support their own weight. When stranded on shore they are helpless.

Fourteen species of whales form the family *Ziphiidae*, the curious Beaked Whales. Most of them have only two teeth, at the very tip of the lower jaw. Typical of this family is Cuvier's Whale which occurs in a number of colour schemes and inhabits the Atlantic and Pacific oceans.

The Bottle-nosed Whale of the same family inhabits the Arctic and Atlantic oceans and migrates to the Mediterranean in winter. A similar species occurs in Australia. Like many large whales this animal feeds largely on squid and cuttlefish.

The Killer Whale (*Delphinidae*) is the most dangerous animal inhabiting the ocean, even more so than the shark. It is carnivorous, hunting in packs of up to fifty for seals, seabirds and smaller whales. It occurs in all oceans but is commonest in Polar areas, where it can break ice one metre thick.

The huge Sperm Whale belongs to the family *Physeteridae* and wanders all over the world. Huge teeth enable it to catch the largest fish and even sharks.

Sei Whale (*top right*)	*Length:*	*up to 18 m.*
Rorqual or Finback (*centre above*)	*Length:*	*up to 24 m.*
Pygmy Right Whale (*centre below*)	*Length:*	*up to 6·5 m.*
Gray Whale (*bottom*)	*Length:*	*up to 15 m.*

The *Mysticeti* or Baleen or Whalebone Whales do not have teeth but instead grow a series of thin plates of horn-like substance which hang from the roof of the huge mouth. There are about 300 of these plates, smooth on the outer edge and frayed out on the inside. This is the whalebone used in commerce. The whole apparatus acts as a giant sieve through which a mass of water containing small, shrimp-like creatures ('krill') is drawn. The whale then closes its mouth and, with its huge tongue acting like a piston, drives out the water. The krill is caught in the sieve and swallowed.

The Sei Whale is one of the four species of Rorquals, which are world-wide. As with all the larger whales they breed only every other year, the calves being very large, about one third the length of the mother. The gestation period is from ten to twelve months.

The Rorqual or Finback is the second largest of the world's whales. The whalebone (or baleen) in its mouth is about one metre long and, like all Rorquals, the throat is grooved, the dorsal fin is small and the blow-hole double. This family (*Balaenopteridae*) is now much hunted, especially since some other species are protected.

Even the smallest Baleen Whale is a giant; the Pygmy Right Whale from southern waters is about three times the length of a tall man.

The Gray Whale, now found only in the North Pacific, belongs to the family *Eschrichtidae* and was once nearly extinct. It is now internationally protected. The world population is about six thousand.

Blue Whale and calf (*top*)

Length:	*up to 30 m.*
Weight:	*up to 112,500 Kg.*

North Atlantic Right Whale (*centre*)

Length:	*up to 18 m.*

Hump-backed Whale (*bottom*)

Length:	*up to 15 m.*

Whales have poor eyesight in air, but it is fairly good under water. Their hearing is excellent and they rely on this to keep in touch with each other when submerged. For this purpose they make a very wide variety of sounds which have been much studied in recent years. From this it seems possible that the smaller whales at least use a system of 'echo-location' rather like that used by ships or by bats*. That is to say, they emit sounds and receive back the echoes from them as a means of detecting objects under water.

There is no doubt that Whales are remarkably intelligent. Unfortunately, thanks to the greediness of commercial whaling, many species are sadly depleted. Some are now protected under international agreements.

The Blue Whale (family *Balaenopteridae*) is the largest mammal that ever lived. Its tongue alone weighs about the same as an elephant, and a new-born calf is more than seven metres long. This marvellous animal was so ruthlessly hunted in the past that it has had to be protected in order to save it from extinction. It occurs in polar waters in summer and migrates towards sub-tropical areas, where it breeds, in winter.

The last family of Whales is the *Balaenidae*, known as 'Right' Whales and so-called because they were once considered the most desirable commercially. They are huge whales of rather stocky build, now increasingly rare.

The North Atlantic Right Whale is one of four similar species found in the cooler waters of the Atlantic and Pacific oceans.

The Hump-back occurs round both polar regions and is now rare and protected.

* *See page 46.*

Dugong

The *Sirenia* is a small order of mammals in which there are four species. They are completely aquatic, as whales are, breeding, sleeping and feeding in the water; and their bodies are fully adapted to the sort of life they lead. But their origins are totally different from those of whales; for it is believed that whales are derived from a carnivorous ancestor while Sirenians are believed to come from a vegetarian source similar to that of the elephants.

The most famous of all Sirenians is perhaps Steller's Sea Cow, a huge animal some seven metres long which was discovered in 1741 in the Bering Sea. By 1768 the whole species was extinct, slaughtered for meat by traders and explorers. Like all Sirenians it was a slow, somewhat stupid animal, quite harmless and defenceless. It is just possible that a very few may still exist, as in 1962 a Russian ship reported a group of huge unidentified sea animals near Cape Navarin.

The Dugong (family *Dugongidae*) occurs on the coast of East Africa and in the Red Sea, Indian Ocean and thence to tropical Australian waters. It is not a common animal and is believed to be decreasing in numbers over most of its range. This may be due to the fact that it is large, easily caught and good to eat – a fatal combination. In Australia it is less rare.

Dugongs have horizontal, notched tails ('flukes') like whales, and the bulls have small tusks. In Steller's Sea Cow the male's tusks were gigantic.

Water vegetation provides all the immense amount of food which Sirenians consume daily.

Manatee

Length: up to 4·5 m.
Weight: up to 360 Kg.

There are three species of Manatee, a *Sirenian* of the family *Trichechidae*. They occur in rivers and coastal waters of the south-eastern United States, in the West Indies, in South America and off the west coast of Africa.

Like the Dugong, this is a completely aquatic animal with solid bones which keep it submerged, and with prehensile lips which help it to grasp water weed. Dugongs live alone or in pairs, but Manatees tend to form groups of about twenty animals. They can stay submerged for about fifteen minutes.

Sirenian calves are born singly after a gestation period of eleven months for the Dugong and six months for the Manatees. Both species are extremely affectionate not only to each other but also to their calves. The birth takes place under water, but the calf is instantly carried to the surface by the mother and kept there for about forty-five minutes. It is then gradually introduced to life under water.

Calves are, in fact, nursed under water, but ancient legends recount how the mother Sirenian stands upright in the water nursing her infant like a human baby. From this it is believed that the legend of mermaids originated.

The Manatee's enormous appetite for water weed has on occasion caused it to be employed for clearing weed from canals in British Guiana.

Like the Dugong, Manatees, which have a rounded tail, are becoming scarcer. Sharks and crocodiles prey upon them, but their chief enemy is man. They produce meat, oil and leather; and in South America their bones are believed to possess magical medicinal properties.

Serotine Bat (*top left*) — *showing flight attitude.*

Big Brown Bat (*centre*) — *showing wing construction.*

Pipistrelle (*bottom right*) — *showing normal resting attitude.*

Frosted Bat (*bottom left*) — *showing resting posture on level surface.*

Bats are the only mammals which are able to fly. It is true that some other mammals, such as the Flying Squirrels, can glide, but Bats achieve true flight by flapping their wings rather in the manner of birds. However, Bats use their hind legs as well as their fore-limbs to move their wings. These are no more than two layers of elastic skin stretched over each side of the arms and hands and extending round the body, feet and tail (A).

The fingers of Bats have been greatly elongated to form struts to support the wing membrane, and their thumbs have evolved into small projecting hooks. On the inner side of each ankle is a 'spur', known as the calcar, which helps to support the membranes round the tail.

The flight of Bats, which includes gliding and hovering, consists of a 'swimming-in-air' motion (B). They cannot soar as most birds can, but by bending their fingers they can alter the shape of the wing in flight, thus acquiring great agility. When at rest the wing is folded away very neatly, and the Bat hangs head downwards from its feet (C).

The hind legs of Bats are twisted round, so that the knees point upwards. This assists both in the flight action and in the resting position. From this head-down posture a Bat can take off by simply letting go with its feet.

Occasionally Bats will rest upon a level surface in the position shown (D) and some species use this attitude for 'walking' on level surfaces. Some Bats while at rest completely enfold themselves in their wings.

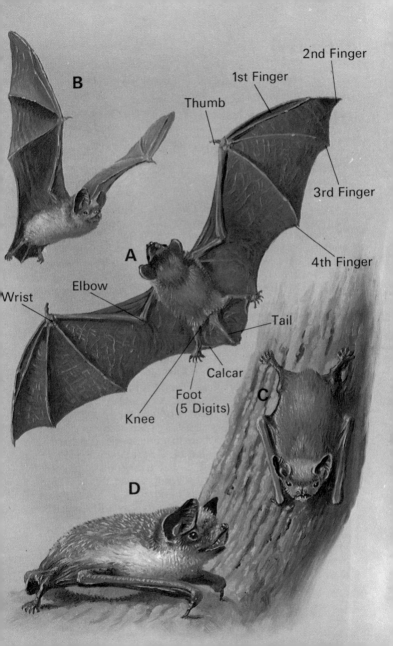

B

2nd Finger

1st Finger

Thumb

3rd Finger

4th Finger

A

Wrist

Elbow

Tail

Calcar

Foot
(5 Digits)

Knee

C

D

Flying Fox	Length, head and body up to 40 cm.
(*centre, and inset right*)	
Short-nosed Fruit Bat (*top right*)	Length, head and body: 12 cm.
Hammer-headed Bat (*inset left*)	Length, head and body: 27 cm.
Tomb Bat (*bottom left*)	Length, head and body up to 10 cm.
Sheath-tailed Bat (*bottom right*)	Length, head and body up to 6 cm.

Bats belong to the order *Chiroptera* which is divided into two sub-orders, *Megachiroptera* which contains one family, the Fruit Bats or *Pteropodidae*; and *Microchiroptera* which contains sixteen families and consists principally of the smaller Bats, many of which are insectivorous. *Chiroptera* is the second largest order of mammals, only exceeded by the Rodents. There are about nine hundred and eighty species.

The principal differences between the two sub-orders is in the shape of the margin of the ear and the size of the eyes. All bats can see, but Fruit Bats have large eyes and use vision very much more than the *Microchiroptera*, locating their food by sight. They feed in the evening and at night on fruit, flowers and, in some cases, on nectar.

Most Fruit Bats, which are found throughout the tropical and sub-tropical parts of Africa, Asia and Australia, live in large groups. Some of them, notably the so-called Flying Foxes, are large animals with a wing span of up to 1.5 metres. Their rather dog-like faces are in some species distorted into grotesque shapes such as that of the Hammer-headed Fruit Bat of equatorial Africa. This bat is also distinguished by having an incredibly loud voice not unlike the croaking of frogs. Altogether there are one hundred and thirty species of Fruit Bats, many of them known from only a few specimens.

The Tomb Bat (*Microchiroptera*), found in Africa, Asia and Australia, belongs to the family *Emballonuridae*, and is often actually found in tombs. This family also contains the tropical Sheath-tailed Bats. Both are principally insectivorous.

Bull-dog Bat (*top left*)   *Length, head and body up to 13 cm.*

Australian False Vampire Bat (*centre right*)   *Length, head and body up to 14 cm.*

Common Vampire Bat (*bottom*)   *Length, head and body up to 9 cm.*

Although the great majority of Bats are fruit or insect eaters, there are others which feed in unexpected ways. Some Bats with specially long tongues probe flowers for the nectar and pollen.

The Bull-dog Bat or Fisherman Bat of South America belongs to the family *Noctilionidae* and is peculiar in that it catches small fish, swooping over the surface of the water and grasping the fish in its exceptionally large feet. The prey is either eaten in flight or taken in cheek pouches to be eaten while roosting. Hunting takes place by day as well as night and over sea as well as fresh water.

False Vampire Bats belong to the family *Megadermatidae*, ranging from central Africa to southern Asia and Australia. Some of them are insectivorous but four species are carnivorous, feeding on small mammals, birds and frogs as well as upon other bats. They are not Vampires (blood drinkers) in the strictest sense.

Vampire Bats (family *Desmodontidae*) occur in three species found in Mexico and South America, all of which live entirely on the fresh blood of other animals.

The Common Vampire Bat usually lives in small, foul-smelling colonies in caves. When hunting it flies low over the ground, alighting near another animal which may be anything from a horse to a roosting bird. The Vampire creeps up to it, bites it with specially sharp front teeth and laps up the blood as it flows. The great danger to the victim is not so much loss of blood but more the fact that Vampires are noted carriers of various diseases, particularly rabies.

Mexican Fruit Bat
(*top right*)

Length, head and body: 6–10 cm.

Mexican Big-eared Bat (*centre*)

Length, head and body: 5–7 cm.

Trident Leaf-nosed Bat (*bottom*)

Length, head and body: 5–6 cm.

Horseshoe Bat
(*top left*)

Length, head and body: 3–10 cm.

The *Microchiroptera* have very poor night vision and rely on a system known as 'echo-location' to guide them in flight, to detect obstructions and pursue their prey. Put very simply, this system consists of the Bat issuing a continuous series of high-pitched sounds at very frequent intervals, the sound waves of which strike objects and rebound. The 'echo' is picked up by the Bat's specially constructed ears and the direction and speed of flight is adjusted accordingly.

Many insectivorous Bats fly with the mouth open, emitting a series of squeaks; but some bats, such as those shown here, keep the mouth closed and emit the sound through the nose, rather as we do when we hum.

These Bats carry elaborate structures on their noses, known as 'nose-leafs', which can be quite simple or extremely complex. A very simple nose-leaf is displayed by the Mexican Fruit Bat, a member of the family *Phyllostomatidae* or American Leaf-nosed Bats of which there are 140 species.

More elaborate is the nose-leaf of the Big-eared Bat of the same family and also from Mexico. It eats insects as well as fruit. The nose-leaf becomes more complicated in the Trident Leaf-nosed Bat (family *Hipposideridae*, the Old World Leaf-nosed Bats). This Bat lives in caves in parts of Africa and also occurs in northern India and Arabia.

Horseshoe Bats, with an extremely complex nose-leaf, belong to the family *Rhinolophidae*. They occur in some fifty species throughout the temperate and tropical areas of Africa and Asia, and also in Britain but not in Scotland.

Long-eared Bat (*top*)   *Length, head and body:*   4–7 cm.

Tube-nosed Bat   *Length, head and body:* 3·5–6 cm.
(*centre above*)

House Bat (*bottom*)   *Length, head and body:* 3·5–7·5 cm.

Free-tailed Bat   *Length, head and body:* 4·5–10 cm.
(*centre below*)

Bats are found all over the world with the exception of the polar regions. In the colder parts of their range hibernation occurs in the winter when the animals' temperature may drop to as little as 8°C, and both breathing and heartbeat become extremely slow. In autumn these Bats become very fat and choose places for hibernation such as caves which are frost-free and permanently damp.

In the warmer parts of the world where food, in the form of fruit or insects, is available throughout the year, hibernation is not necessary.

The largest Bat family is the *Vespertilionidae*, containing about 275 species distributed throughout the world, most of which are insectivorous.

Long-eared Bats belong to this family and are found in temperate regions throughout the world. They often hover in the manner of a humming bird, and moths are their principal prey.

Another member of this family is the curious Tube-nosed Bat whose nostrils are placed at the end of tubes. Ten species occur in India, much of Asia including Japan, New Guinea and the Philippines.

The *Vespertilionidae* (meaning 'Evening' Bats) fly with the mouth open, emitting sounds so high that they are inaudible to human ears. Included in this family is the very common House Bat which ranges throughout tropical and temperate Asia. Three species occur in Africa. They usually roost in palm trees but are also found in houses.

The peculiar Free-tailed Bats belong to the family *Molossidae* and occur in the warmer parts of the world including southern Europe. Millions of them are sometimes found roosting in caves.

Natterer's Bat (*top*)	*Length, head and body:* 4–5 cm.
Pipistrelle (*centre above*)	*Length, head and body:* 3·5–10 cm.
Noctule (*centre below*)	*Length, head and body:* 5–10 cm.
Barbastelle (*bottom*)	*Length, head and body:* up to 6 cm.

Bats usually produce their young singly. In colder climates they mate in the autumn, but the female egg cell is not fertilised at once, the male sperm remaining within the female until after hibernation is over, when 'delayed fertilisation' occurs. A similar process, known as 'delayed implantation' takes place in other mammals such as Badgers, Seals, Martens, some Otters and Roe Deer. In warmer climates 'delayed fertilisation' does not occur and bats probably breed every six months.

Young Bats are carried by their mothers for some weeks and are suckled just like any other mammal. They can fly at a very early age.

The Bats shown here are all members of the family *Vespertilionidae* and all occur in Britain.

Natterer's Bat is one of about sixty species of Little Brown Bats or Mouse-eared Bats which have a world wide distribution.

The Pipistrelle is also world-wide and the forty species range from very small to medium sized. In Britain this is the commonest bat and is sometimes seen in daylight, hawking for gnats.

Noctules are also seen in daylight and their range, which is throughout Asia and Europe, extends quite far north. Like many other Bats they migrate over considerable distances in order to find suitable hibernation sites.

The Barbastelle is not very common, occurring in two species only in western Asia and Europe. The ears are joined above the crown of the head, a feature shared with other species such as the Long-eared Bat and the False Vampire Bat.

INDEX